PEOPLES AND THEIR ENVIRONMENTS ™

# PEOPLES OF THE DESERT

Robert Low

The Rosen Publishing Group's

**PowerKids Press™**

New York

Published in 1996 by The Rosen Publishing Group, Inc.
29 East 21st Street, New York, NY 10010

Copyright © 1996 by The Rosen Publishing Group, Inc.

First Edition

Book design: Erin McKenna and Kim Sonsky

Photo credits: Cover, pp. 4, 15 © J. P. Valentin/ANAKO Editions; p. 7 © Adria LaViolette; p. 8 © Royal Geographical Society; p. 11 © H. Lam Duc/ANAKO Editions; p. 12 © Philippe Frey/Gamma Liaison; p. 16 © Gille Martin/Gamma Liaison Network; p. 19 © F. Boussouf/ANAKO Editions; p. 20 © Weinberg–South Light/Gamma Liaison.

Low, Robert, 1952–
        Peoples of the desert / Robert Low.
            p.        cm. — (Peoples and their environments)
        Includes index.
        Summary: An introduction to the natural wonders of the desert and two peoples who live there, the San and the Tuareg.
        ISBN 0-8239-2296-0
        1. San (African people)—Social life and customs—Juvenile literature. 2. Tuaregs—Social life and customs—Juvenile literature. 3. Desert ecology—Sahara—Juvenile literature. 4. Desert ecology—Kalahari Desert—Juvenile literature. [1. San (African people). 2. Tuaregs. 3. Desert ecology. 4. Ecology.] I. Title. II. Series: Low Robert, 1952– Peoples and their environments.
        DT1058.S36L69 1996
        966'.004961—dc20                                         96-7753
                                                                    CIP
                                                                    AC

Manufactured in the United States of America

# Contents

# What Is a Desert?

A **desert** (DEH-zert) is a large area of dry land. In some deserts, the land is covered with sand. Other deserts are covered with dirt or rocks.

Deserts have long dry seasons and short rainy seasons. During the rainy season, it often rains every day. Small rivers and lakes may appear. But the land is so dry that it soaks up all the water after the rain stops. The months between rainy seasons can seem very long.

Deserts are hot during the day and cool, or even cold, at night.

◀ Deserts receive very little rain.

# The Peoples of the Desert

It may seem as if nothing can live in the desert because it is so hot and dry. But many groups of people do live there. Two of these peoples are the **Tuareg** (TWA-reg) and the **San** (SAN). The Tuareg live in the **Sahara** (suh-HARE-ah) Desert in Northwest Africa. The San live in the **Kalahari** (kah-lah-HAH-ree) Desert in Southern Africa. Like people everywhere, those who live in the desert must have water to survive. The Tuareg and the San move from place to place in search of water. People who move a lot are called **nomads** (NO-madz).

Trade across the desert has led to the building of large, important cities. ▶

# Life on the Move

The San move about once a month, or whenever the water in their area runs out. They travel on foot in groups of about ten families.

The Tuareg move when they run out of water and plants and grass for their goats, sheep, cows, and camels to graze. They travel in groups of four or five families. The men ride camels. The women and children ride donkeys or goats.

Both peoples carry water from one place to the next, so that they and their animals will have enough for the trip.

◀ Groups who live in the desert have to move often to look for food and water.

# Plants and Animals

A variety of plants grow in the desert. **Cacti** (KAK-ty), grasses, bushes, and trees all grow during the rainy season.

Many desert animals need little water to survive. The camels that live in the Sahara store water in the humps on their backs. They can live as long as three months without drinking water. Other animals, such as the **antelopes** (AN-tel-oaps) that live in the Kalahari, need water more often. They seek new sources of water when their waterholes run dry.

Many groups who live in or near the desert use camels for transportation. ▶

# Desert Food

The San once hunted wild animals and gathered their food. Now the laws in Southern Africa don't allow them to travel as freely as they once did. Some San have begun to raise cattle instead. Others work on farms owned by neighboring peoples. The San eat beef and the meat of the few wild animals they still hunt. They also gather fruit, nuts, berries, and vegetables that grow in the desert.

The Tuareg eat grains, such as **millet** (MIL-et), rice, and wheat. They also eat the meat of their cows, goats, and sheep. They drink camel milk and a sweet mint tea.

◀ This San hunter prepared his dinner from the food that he hunted.

# CLOTHING

Both the San and the Tuareg wear clothes that are comfortable in the desert. Many San wear clothes and sandals made from animal skins. Some wear shirts and pants much like the shirts and pants you wear.

Tuareg men wear pants and loosely draped cloths. They also wear **veils** (VAILZ) over their heads and mouths. A man is known by the way he wraps his veil. Tuareg women wear long loose dresses made of woven and dyed cloth.

Tuareg men begin wearing veils when they are about 20 years old. ▶

# Homes

The San and the Tuareg live in homes that can be built quickly and easily since they move so often. The San build their homes from branches laced with twigs. They make roofs out of **thatched** (THACHT) grass. Their homes are usually flat on one side and rounded on the other.

Many Tuareg live in tents made out of animal skins and wooden poles that they carry with them. Today, some Tuareg use tents made of plastic.

◀ Desert homes can be built quickly.

# Families and Communities

The San travel in groups. One group may not see another group for many months. Each member relies on the others in his or her group for support and help. When hunters kill a large animal, they share the meat with everyone in the group.

The Tuareg live and travel in small groups. Tuareg women set up the tents when they arrive at a new place. Tuareg men take care of the animals. Once Tuareg children become teenagers, they help with the chores, such as building or repairing tents or tending the herds.

Tuareg teens usually help tend the animals. ▶

# Children of the Desert

Just as men and women who live in the desert have different jobs, so do children.

Tuareg girls learn how to build and set up tents, cook millet, weave mats, and gather fruit. Boys learn how to tend herds of smaller animals such as goats and sheep. They may also help their fathers care for the camels.

San girls learn how to gather and prepare food. Boys learn how to hunt wild animals.

◀ San boys learn how to hunt with bows and arrows.

# Changing Lives

The Sahara Desert was faced with a severe **drought** (DROWT) over 25 years ago. This drought killed thousands of Tuareg people and their animals. Today, many Tuareg live in cities or **refugee** (REF-yoo-jee) camps. Because of the laws of Northwest Africa, they are no longer free to wander the deserts. Many San have also been forced to give up their nomadic ways.

Despite this, the Tuareg and the San try to continue to follow their **traditions** (truh-DISH-unz). The San and the Tuareg are proud of their past and of their ways.

# Glossary

**antelope** (AN-tel-oap)  Deerlike animal that lives in Africa.

**cacti** (KAK-ty)  Prickly desert plants.

**desert** (DEH-zert)  Large area of dry land.

**drought** (DROWT)  Long period of time without rain.

**Kalahari** (kah-lah-HAH-ree)  Desert in Southern Africa.

**millet** (MIL-et)  Kind of grain.

**nomad** (NO-mad)  One who moves from place to place.

**refugee** (REF-yoo-jee)  Person taking shelter from a natural disaster such as a drought.

**Sahara** (suh-HARE-ah)  Desert in Northwest Africa.

**San** (SAN)  Group of people who live in the Kalahari Desert.

**thatch** (THACH)  Tightly woven grass or leaves.

**tradition** (truh-DISH-un)  Beliefs and practices of a group of people.

**Tuareg** (TWA-reg)  Group of people who live in the Sahara Desert.

**veil** (VAIL)  Piece of cloth worn over a person's face or head.

# Index